☛ Three Tenners ☛

Three ten-minute youth plays

"Raiders of the Lost Rakasa"

"The Witch Makes Five"

and

"Mrs. Calapooza and the Culebra"

by
John Glass

john@studentplays.org

<u>Copyright information. Please read!</u>

☞ About Student Plays ☜

Student Plays consists of **John Glass, Jackie Jernigan,** and **Dominic Torres.** We are a group of playwrights and directors that have written scripts for elementary school through college. *Student Plays* is proud of the variety of ages that our scripts serve.

We are particularly proud of our "creepy" plays, and also our *Latino-themed* plays. These are scripts that focus on Latino youth and the Latino experience. Any school can perform a Latino-themed play: it just requires a general introduction and basic exposure to the Spanish language, something that most schools and students already have.

To contact *Student Plays* or to communicate with one of the playwrights, simply email us at john@studentplays.org.

Raiders of the Lost Rakasa

-

A one-act play

by

John Glass

☞   ☞

Raiders of the Lost Rakasa

<u>Characters</u>

HUNTER   Male. Adventurer. Leader
                     of the group.

CHRISTINE   Female. Adventurer.

MILTON   Male. Adventurer.

JENNY   Female. Adventurer.

LAMONICA   Female. Easily scared.

JOHN   Male. Easily scared.

SALLY   Female. Easily scared.

This ten-minute play is written for grades **five through eight.** The time is the present, the setting a large cave, somewhere far away. On the far side of the stage should be a simple pedestal or small altar, perhaps two or three feet high, with the "Rakasa" on top.

The Rakasa is simply a book, wrapped in gold or silver paper; it, however, should *look* like a sacred idol. Once it is wrapped, the shape should not resemble a book.

On the other side of the stage is an entry-way into the "cave." The entry-way can be an easy arrangement of aluminum/plastic or pvc-tubing, four to five feet wide, draped in cobwebs or old torn sheets.

All of the characters are dressed in adventurer/ explorer clothing, such as safari khakis, boots, straw fedoras, satchels, etc. CHRISTINE should have a small bag of sand.

An assortment of toy rubber snakes are needed for this play.

(At RISE: The group is just outside the entry to the cave, about to enter.)

HUNTER: Okay. This is it! The entrance to the great Rakasa!

LAMONICA: Yeah! This is where the other guys cashed in.

JOHN: Huh? Who?

MILTON: You know, the other guys. The great explorers.

CHRISTINE: Pierre Pancake! José Javalina! Lana the Lasso!

SALLY: Oh yeah. Those dudes. But are we *all* going to go in there?

HUNTER: Of course. Come on.

LAMONICA: Uh . . . I'll stay here.

MILTON: What? Are you serious?

LAMONICA: Yep. I'll stand guard.

JENNY: Why??

LAMONICA: You know. In case someone comes.

JOHN: Me too.

CHRISTINE: You guys are scared!

SALLY: Yep. Hey, guilty as charged. I *know* I'm scared. I'm staying here too.

HUNTER: But come on! This is the Rakasa we're talking about!

SALLY: I don't care if it's all the lemon pie on the planet. It looks creepy in there.

JOHN: Very creepy!

LAMONICA: Yep.

MILTON: Okay. Whatever. *(To the others.)* You guys ready?

HUNTER: Yes!

JENNY: Let's do this. Come on!

HUNTER: Okay . . . here we go.

LAMONICA: I'll say a prayer!

JOHN: I'll say two!

SALLY: I'll say three!

CHRISTINE: Oh, hush!!

>   *(They enter the cave slowly. LAMONICA,
>   JOHN, and SALLY all quietly exit.)*

JENNY: Wow. It's dark.

MILTON: No kidding.

HUNTER: Okay . . . go slow. Easy.

CHRISTINE: I can't believe I traveled 4000 miles for
this.

MILTON: I know. Mosquito bites. Mud and sweat!

JENNY: No hot baths. No television!

CHRISTINE: No "Desperate Housewives"!

HUNTER: Stop! Come on, look. *(Pointing ahead.)*
Do you guys see it?

CHRISTINE: Yep. Is that it?

HUNTER: That's it! The great Rasaka! Come on. Be careful where you walk. Don't step in the red areas.

JENNY: Why not?

HUNTER: Because if you do, poison darts will fly out of the walls!

MILTON: What??

HUNTER: Come on, didn't you see the movie??

CHRISTINE: Oh, yeah! The poison darts.

HUNTER: Come on, keep moving.

JENNY: This is not what I bargained for!!

MILTON: No kidding!
        (Beat. He notices something on the floor.)
Wait . . . what is that?

JENNY: It's . . . oh no.

MILTON: It's . . .

HUNTER: *(With great anguish.)* Snakes. Why did it have to be snakes??

CHRISTINE: Ohh!!

MILTON: Uggh!

HUNTER: Wisconsin vipers. Very dangerous.

JENNY: Go around them!

(They begin to do so.)

MILTON: That one is huge!!

HUNTER: Careful!

CHRISTINE: Ugghhh!

HUNTER: Okay . . . boy, those things are ugly.

MILTON: Yes they are!

JENNY: *(Focusing on the Rakasa.)* Look: there it is! The great Rakasa!

HUNTER: Okay, we have to grab it carefully . . . do you have that bag, Christine?

CHRISTINE: *(Hands him the bag of sand)* Yep. Right here.

HUNTER: Okay. Wow . . . here we go.

MILTON: Yes! We are finally doing this!

JENNY: I know!

HUNTER: *(Preparing to swap the Rakasa with the bag of sand)* Okay . . . one . . two . . three . .

> *(Pause as he swaps the two. Everybody breathes a sigh of relief.)*

CHRISTINE: That's it!

MILTON: Yeah! You did it!

JENNY: I can't believe it was that easy!

HUNTER: I know! Wow!

> *(A low rumbling noise is suddenly heard. The sound quickly becomes louder.)*

HUNTER: Wait . . maybe it *wasn't* that easy!

CHRISTINE: What is that noise? What's happening?

JENNY: The temple is coming down!

MILTON: No!!

HUNTER: Go! Run!

CHRISTINE: Aghh!

(They all run back to the entrance, screaming, dodging the snakes, diving and tumbling through the entry to the cave. LAMONICA, JOHN, and SALLY run over to meet them.)

MILTON: Agghhhh!!!

CHRISTINE: Ohhh!!

HUNTER: Boy, they don't come any closer than that.

JENNY: Amen to that!!

JOHN: Guys! What happened??

JENNY: The temple came crashing down!

MILTON: Yeah, it was epic!

SALLY: You guys got the Rakasa?

HUNTER: Yep. Right here.

SALLY: Sweet!

LAMONICA: Wow, there it is.

JOHN: Man! The Rakasa!

(HUNTER begins to remove the paper/ wrapping.)

SALLY: What are you doing?

HUNTER: I'm opening it! What do you think I'm doing??

JENNY: That, uh, comes off . . ?

HUNTER: Yep.

LAMONICA: Whaa . . ?

JOHN: Okay, this does *not* look good.

MILTON: What is that? It's . . . *español*?

JENNY: Huh?

SALLY: A Spanish book?

HUNTER: Si! The great Rakasa! Aquí está! A Spanish book! Mira . . .
(Opening it, reading the inside.)
"Ándele. Buenas tardes. Por favor!!"

CHRISTINE: We came 4000 miles for *this*?

MILTON: A Spanish book?

HUNTER: Not *just* a Spanish book! The Rakasa!!

JOHN: I can't believe this!

SALLY: Does anybody else want to strangle him besides me??

LAMONICA: *(Suddenly sees something in the distance.)* Guys, look!

CHRISTINE: What?

JOHN: *(Also looking off in the distance.)* Who is that?

HUNTER: The Indians!

JENNY: Who??

HUNTER: The Indians!! This is the part where they chase us!!

LAMONICA: Oh yeah! Come on, let's get out of here! Back to the plane!

HUNTER: Run!

> *(Everyone except for JOHN begins to flee in the same direction.)*

JENNY & **SALLY:** Agghhh!!

CHRISTINE: Go! Go!

MILTON: To the airplane!

JOHN: Guys?? Wait!!

(They all stop and turn to face JOHN.)

CHRISTINE: What?

SALLY: What is it??

HUNTER: Come on!! Hurry!

JOHN: *(Pointing in the other direction.)* The plane is THAT WAY!!

ALL except for JOHN: AGGHHH!!

(They begin to run in the other direction, stumbling and screaming. End of play.)

The Witch Makes Five

-

A one-act play

by
John Glass

The Witch Makes Five

Characters of the Play

JOYCE	High School Student. Distraught. Agitated.
ROD	High School Student. Nervous.
STACIE	High School Student. Nervous.
WORKER 1	Either gender. Small role at the play's end.
WORKER 2	Either gender. Small role at the play's end.

The setting is a patient's room in a mental treatment center for the youth. JOYCE is a patient and is being visited by ROD and STACIE. She is wearing a hospital/facility gown or shirt. There are a few chairs, a small table with a telephone, and if possible, a bed or cot. Everyone is shaken and somewhat uncomfortable.

The time is the present, October, and there are several Halloween decorations hanging about. A witch face should be one of the decorations, prominently displayed.

This ten-minute spooky play is best suited for **middle school** or **high school.** The few allusions to "high school student" and so forth can easily be altered.

At RISE: ROD and JOYCE are seated, in the middle of discussion.

ROD: Well, I'll tell you one thing.

JOYCE: What?

ROD: I'm never going camping again.

JOYCE: Man. No kidding!

ROD: And I'm also never going to go looking for *anything* in the middle of the woods. Stupid *StoneHouse* . . .

JOYCE: Well, let's be honest: something tells me the StoneHouse found *us*.

ROD: Tell me about it *(Beat.)* But you know what was really cool?

JOYCE: What?

ROD: Those wicked-looking pine trees! In the moonlight!

JOYCE: Don't start with the pine trees!

ROD: Seriously, Joyce. I wasn't going to mention it. But the way those needles silhouetted against the moon! Wow . . .

JOYCE: You are such a writer.

ROD: Come on, it was beautiful. We've got to find something positive out of all this. Right?

JOYCE: Um, I guess.

ROD: It was exotic.

JOYCE: Look. I don't want us to keep ignoring this. You know what we saw. Don't you?

ROD: Well . . . *(Uncomfortably)* I know what I *think* I saw.

JOYCE: You mean, you *know* what you saw.

ROD: Hmmph.

JOYCE: Come on, Stacie saw her too. Let's not pretend. Okay?

ROD: *(Quietly.)* Yeah. I know.

JOYCE: We all saw her. *(Beat. She is very distraught.)* But . . . Rod?

ROD: What?

JOYCE: You know what I absolutely *can't* pretend about that camping trip? I know we agreed to drop this for now. But Rod . . . there were four of us out there. *Four* of us!

ROD: Look, Joyce—

> *(Enter STACIE, carrying a small bottle/can of juice. She sets it down.)*

JOYCE: *(Grabbing him by the arm.)* I know, I know. You guys think I lost it out in those woods. Both of you do!

ROD: I didn't say that!

STACIE: *(Groaning, at hearing the discussion)* Ughh!

JOYCE: But it was you, me, Stacie . . . and *Scottie*! Scottie was the one that organized the whole camping trip!

ROD: Joyce—

JOYCE: You guys have known him since that film class our freshman year! And I've known him for almost that long!

STACIE: Joyce? We know that you—

JOYCE: Oh, don't start, Stacie. I know what you're thinking! You've already said that I belong in here. That this place might be good for me for a little while.

STACIE: You know that I didn't mean it like that! Come on!

JOYCE: Whatever.

ROD: Joyce, it's just that we've already told you. We don't know a *Scottie!* We never have! It was you, Stacie and me! Three college idiots in the middle of the woods!

STACIE: Searching for something we never should have been looking for.

ROD: *(Slowly.)* Something . . *happened* out there, Joyce. Something really bizarre.

STACIE: Right.

ROD: Something that affected you.

JOYCE: Stacie, you believe that we saw something. Don't you?

(Pause. STACIE sits, and speaks slowly.)

STACIE: Oh, yeah. Absolutely. I told you that I did. That face . . . I can't get it out of my brain.

JOYCE: Okay. So if you remember that, don't you remember how Scottie walked right up to that window? Holding that flashlight?? Scottie was the first one to see her!!

STACIE: Joyce, that didn't happen! *Rod* was holding the flashlight! There *was* no Scottie! There were only *three* of us out there, Joyce.

JOYCE: There were FOUR OF US!! Us three, and *Scottie*!!
    (Pause.)
And that . . that *witch*. The witch makes five.
    (Off their look.)
Don't look at me like that!

ROD: Joyce, take your medication.

JOYCE: Ughhh.

STACIE: Yeah, here's the juice.

JOYCE: I don't have the pills yet. The nurse should be bringing them in a minute.

ROD: Okay. Well . . . relax. You're okay.

JOYCE: And anyway, I need water. The doctor said not to take medication with juice.

ROD: I'll go get some water.

STACIE: Sorry, I'll get it.

ROD: No, it's fine, I got it. There's a fountain down the hall.

JOYCE: There are cups in the nurse's office.

ROD: Be right back.

JOYCE: Thanks, Rod.

(Pause as he exits. JOYCE attempts to collect herself.)

JOYCE: I'm sorry, Stacie.

STACIE: It's okay. Just try and stay calm.

JOYCE: I know. I know.

STACIE: You'll be out of this place in no time.

JOYCE: I hope . . . *(Pause. She sighs, looks around the room.)* Damn. Do they have to have these stupid Halloween decorations in here?

STACIE: Well, it *is* October.

JOYCE: I know . . . but sheesh. I'm already freaked out as it is.
(Beat. Still distraught.)
I apologize, Stacie. I'm just a wreck.

STACIE: It's fine.

JOYCE: No, I'm really a wreck. I'm eighteen years old and I had a nervous breakdown. What teenager does that?
(Beat.)
And my parents, wow, they're all upset. I had to practically beg them to leave this afternoon, to get away for a few hours. To go grab some dinner.

STACIE: I talked to your teachers. They all know you'll be out of school for a bit.

JOYCE: Aggh! My classes!

STACIE: It's fine. They understood. You'll be out of here soon. Your teachers don't know *exactly* what you're going through but they know that it's serious.

JOYCE: Well, what we went through *was* serious.

STACIE: Gosh . . . don't remind me. It's . . . the *explaining* part that's eventually going to be tough. For *all* of us.

(Pause as they reflect.)

JOYCE: I can still see her. Her face. Uggh. Those wrinkled, bony hands, holding that candle. So vicious and dark.

STACIE: *(Slowly.)* Nobody knows, Joyce. Nobody.

JOYCE: What??

STACIE: I didn't tell anyone. About her.

JOYCE: Are you serious? No one??

STACIE: I mean . . . how can I? My parents don't know, or anyone else. I don't know if I'll ever tell a single person. *(Slowly.)* I just don't want to . . .

JOYCE: . . end up in here like I did?

STACIE: No. I didn't say that.

JOYCE: Well. You don't *have* to. It's all over your face.

STACIE: I'm sorry. I–

JOYCE: *(Holding a hand up.)* Don't. It's fine. I understand.

> *(Pause. They gather themselves, uncomfortably.)*

STACIE: Okay. Well. Yeah. Stupid StoneHouse.

JOYCE: I know . . .

STACIE: Stupid witch.

> *(Beat. JOYCE attempts to lighten things up.)*

JOYCE: And Rod! Ha! Rod screamed like a little girl!

> *(Pause as she laughs. STACIE stares at her in confusion.)*

STACIE: Who . . ?

JOYCE: *Rod,* Stacie. Our friend.

STACIE: Who the heck are you talking about?

JOYCE: ROD!! *(She jumps up and paces in anger.)* Oh, what is HAPPENING here?? First Scottie, and now Rod??

STACIE: Joyce—

JOYCE: He's our *friend*, Stacie! He's down the hall, getting water for my medication!

STACIE: Who are you talking about?? Nobody came to visit you but me!!

JOYCE: You came with Rod!! Our goofball writer friend!! *Rod,* Stacie! We went camping with him this weekend!!

STACIE: Joyce, I don't know a *Rod!* Or a *Scottie!* You and me went camping, and you and me *only.*

JOYCE: No!

STACIE: Joyce, get a grip of yourself!

JOYCE: I've *got* a grip of myself! It's everybody else I'm worried about!! *(Tears down the witch decoration.)* I should have taken that down a long time ago!

STACIE: Look, I'm going to call one of the nurses.
　　　(Moves to pick up the phone.)

JOYCE: *(Calling down the hallway.)* ROD?? Rod, get in here! Rod!!

STACIE: *(On phone)* Hello . .? Hello! I need help in Room 8!

JOYCE: ROD!

(She exits, calling his name.)

STACIE: Joyce, come back! *(Back on phone.)* Hello? Is anyone there?? Hello??
(Pause.)
Oh, yes, I am in room 8, and I really need your help! The patient here just ran out!
(Pause.)
What?? What do you mean, *there's no patient in this room*?? Joyce Carol is in this room! Room 8!
(Pause. She repeats herself.)
Her name is Joyce Carol! I'm here visiting her! Hello? Did you hear me?? HELLO??
(Slams the phone down. She turns to the hall way, and begins to exit.)
JOYCE?? JOYCE!!

(She runs out, calling her name. Long pause. Enter two workers from the <u>other</u> side of the stage. They are carrying a broom, cleaning materials, and a clipboard with papers.)

WORKER ONE: You brought the dustpan, didn't you?

WORKER TWO: Yep. Right here.

WORKER ONE: Okay. Nobody's been in here for a few days so it's probably a little dusty.

WORKER TWO: Can't believe how quiet it's been all day.

WORKER ONE: I know. It's like a ghost town.

WORKER TWO: I wish it were always this quiet.
        (Pause.)
How many do we have left to clean?

WORKER ONE: Two more. But they want this room ready by the morning, for a new patient.

WORKER TWO: Yeah.

WORKER ONE: *(Picking up the witch decoration.)*
Looks like one of the decorations fell off the wall.

WORKER TWO: Ugghh. I've never liked witches.

WORKER ONE: Ha. I've always liked them. This needs to go back on the wall.

WORKER TWO: Mmmm. If you say so . . .

> *(They continue working in silence. Lights fade. End of play.)*

Mrs. Calapooza and the Culebra

-

A one-act play

by
John Glass

☞   ☞

Mrs. Calapooza and the Culebra

Characters

MRS. CALAPOOZA A teacher, in her sixties or seventies. Stern, grouchy. Played by an adult or a student with a wig and proper clothing.

KATIE A student. Aggressive. Feisty.

LUKE A student. Kind.

ISABELLA A student. Passive.

SIMONE A student. Kind.

This ten-minute play is designed for grades **five through eight.** The time is the present, the place a classroom, during a Spanish quiz. The students are seated at tables or in desks, and Mrs. Calapooza is at her desk/table, going through various papers. She has a large bag or purse beside her desk. There should be some distance between her and the others.

There are Spanish words and phrases woven throughout the play but students of any race or ethnicity can do the play. The names of the characters may be changed, giving flexibility to the gender of each character. Any gender can play any of the characters.

(AT RISE: A school day. All four students are in the class, furiously studying. MRS. CALAPOOZA is at her desk, looking at various papers.)

KATIE: Agghh! I'm so tired of these Spanish quizzes!

ISABELLA: I know. So many words!

LUKE: Mrs. Calapooza drives me bananas.

SIMONE: Mantequilla.

LUKE: What?

SIMONE: You said 'bananas.' It's *mantequilla*, in Spanish.

KATIE: Bananas is *plátanos*, you dope.

LUKE: No, I thought bananas was *bananas*.

ISABELLA: I think it's both.

SIMONE: Oh, right. Mantequilla is *butter*. Sorry.

LUKE: Well, whatever. *(Looking back at his notes.)* Aghh! I'm not ready for this!

ISABELLA: Me neither!!

KATIE: Well, don't worry. I took care of our little situation. Ha, ha . . .

SIMONE: Really?

ISABELLA: Did you hide it??

KATIE: Yes! It's all taken care of!
   (She points in MRS. CALAPOOZA's direction.)
Right up there!

MRS. CALAPOOZA: Okay, class. *(Gets up, walks over and begins to hand out the quiz papers.)* Let's begin!

LUKE: *(To KATIE.)* I can't believe you!!

KATE: Sshhh!!

MRS. CALAPOOZA: Listos??

SIMONE: Can we have a little more time to study?

MRS. CALAPOOZA: NO! Put all papers away.

ISABELLA: Ohhh!

MRS. CALAPOOZA: Now!

LUKE: Okay! Okay!

MRS. CALAPOOZA: Let's begin. Ready? Número uno . . . pastel!

(Pause. They all fidget, trying to remember.)

MRS. CALAPOOZA: Pastel!
   (Pause.)
Número dos . . . cebolla!

ISABELLA: Ohhh . . what is cebolla?

MRS. CALAPOOZA: Silencio! NO TALKING DURING THE QUIZ!!

ISABELLA: Sorry!

MRS. CALAPOOZA: Cebolla!
   (Pause.)
Número tres . . . zanahoria.

KATIE: Aghh! I forgot that word!

MRS. CALAPOOZA: Sounds like a personal problem.

KATIE: Uhhhh . . .

MRS. CALAPOOZA: Zanahoria!
   (Pause.)
Número cuatro . . . naranja!

SIMONE: Mrs. Calapooza, my pencil lead broke.

MRS. CALAPOOZA: Too bad! You should have come prepared!

SIMONE: But—

MRS. CALAPOOZA: Naranja!
(Pause.)
Número cinco . . .

ISABELLA: Hang on!

MRS. CALAPOOZA: Papas!

LUKE: Uh, does that mean 'daddies'?

MRS. CALAPOOZA: It's going to mean an F if you don't be quiet!

LUKE: Oops! Sorry!

MRS. CALAPOOZA: Papas!
(Pause.)
Okay, there's one more . . . pepino!
(Pause. They continue to fidget and think.)
Pepino! Okay, your time is up!

KATIE: Already??

SIMONE: Is that it??

MRS. CALAPOOZA: Sí! You heard me! Pass me all the papers.

KATIE: Wow . . .

MRS. CALAPOOZA: *(As she collects them.)* Gracias . . gracias . . .

SIMONE: *(Still dazed.)* Good Lord . . .

MRS. CALAPOOZA: Gracias.

> *(The bell rings. They all get up slowly to exit. MRS. CALAPOOZA walks back to her desk. She eventually goes over to her bag.)*

MRS. CALAPOOZA: Hasta luego, clase.

ISABELLA: Bye.

LUKE: Hasta luego.

> *(Pause as they all come together, depressed, to talk.)*

SIMONE: Man! She is so mean!

KATIE: And did you see how fast she went on that quiz?

LUKE: I know! No time at all!

ISABELLA: It's just crazy. They should have hired somebody else for Spanish.

SIMONE: I know. Someone like that guy Mr. Glass.

ISABELLA: Yeah! He rocked.

LUKE: Guys . . . look. She's getting her bag!

ISABELLA: Is she?

KATIE: There she goes! This is it!

(MRS. CALAPOOZA opens her bag, pulls out a large rubber snake and screams, throwing it up in the air in horror. She grabs her chest and falls to the ground. The students all gasp and shriek.)

KATIE: We did it! The culebra always wins!

ISABELLA: What are you talking about it?? You may have given her a heart attack!!

(They all run over to her.)

SIMONE: Mrs. Calapooza!!

LUKE: Mrs. Calapooza!

(They lean down over her.)

ISABELLA: Mrs. Calapooza, can you hear us? Are you okay?

(Long pause. Nothing.)

KATIE: Oh, what have we done??

SIMONE: We need to give her CPR!!

KATIE: Uh . . .CPR?

(They all cringe and look at each other.)

LUKE: Uhhh . . .

ISABELLA: Uhh . . .

LUKE: Mrs. Calapooza??

SIMONE: Mrs. Calapooza . . . can you hear us??

(She quickly opens her eyes and looks right at them.)

MRS. CALAPOOZA: Of course I can hear you!
(Sitting up.)

ISABELLA: Agghh!

KATIE: Ohhh!

MRS. CALAPOOZA: What do you think I am? Deaf?
(Standing up quickly.)

LUKE: So you're . . . okay?

ISABELLA: You didn't have a heart attack?

MRS. CALAPOOZA: I was fooling the whole time!

SIMONE: Ah, man!

MRS. CALAPOOZA: That's right! I know you guys put that rubber snake in there! That *culebra*! The question is . . . *who?*

KATIE: *(Pointing at LUKE.)* He did it!

LUKE: No, she did! *(Pointing at ISABELLA.)*

ISABELLA: I didn't do it!!

MRS. CALAPOOZA: So, who's lying then? Huh? *All* of you??

KATIE: No!!

SIMONE & LUKE: No!!

ISABELLA: *I'm* not lying!!

MRS. CALAPOOZA: Get out of here!! All of you! You're gonna be late for class!!

(They all run out of the class.)

MRS. CALAPOOZA: Go!! And don't you ever try a trick like that again!! Do you hear me? EVER!!

(Pause. She picks up the snake and plays with it. She faces the audience, lightly laughing, in an evil-like manner.)

MRS. CALAPOOZA: Culebra, culebra, my little culebra . . . don't these kiddies know? Teachers always know. Yes, that's right. We always know!

(She smiles at the snake as she sits down and begins to grade papers. End of play.)

☞ More from Student Plays ☜

Othello's Just Another Fellow

Dramedy. **Grades 5-7.** 25-35 minutes. 8 actors: 4 males, 3 females, one teacher (or student portraying a teacher) 3 to 5 extras, if needed. ****A Latino-themed play****

A group of students are involved in a school production of *Othello*, but one of them is disturbed about the lack of diversity in the play. He takes certain steps to disrupt the play but in the end is encouraged by the others to try and make a difference in another, more constructive way. A lesson is learned, and the production is saved from disaster!

Pagasqueeny's Pantry

Comedy. **Middle/High School.** 15-20 minutes. 6 actors: 3 females, 2 males. One student (or a teacher) plays the comical role of the elderly Mr. Pagasqueeny.

Three friends sneak into Mr. Pagasqueeny's home to get something that one of them left behind. But in walks Pagasqueeny and they must hide in the pantry! In this comical play, a lesson is learned about honesty and trust, but it takes a heated discussion in the pantry and a subsequent attempt to escape to find this out!

Una Carta de Abuelo

Dramedy. **Middle/High School.** 35-45 minutes. 10 actors: 1 teacher, 5 females, 4 males. (With the option of 4-5 extra actors in two scenes.) ****A Latino-themed play****

Two cousins discover an old letter in their late grandfather's comic collection that they think leads to treasure! The cousins often butt heads, with one believing that he is more "Mexican," the other believing that some people make too much of a fuss about "being Mexican." Thus, they form their *own* groups in search of what Grandpa hid long ago. But what they find is actually worth more than merely silver or gold.

Barbecue at the Prom!

Dramedy. **Grades 5-8.** 25-35 minutes. 6 actors: 3 females, 3 males

It's a classic tale of guys versus girls! It's a prom committee, and everybody is supposed to work together but differences and opinions get in the way, causing the guys and girls to form their groups. For the end-of-the-year prom, one side wants pasta and lace, the other wants sports and barbecue! The two groups square off but eventually work together, demonstrating the importance of cooperation and compromise.

Going to Guatemala

Dramedy. **High School.** 50-60 minutes. 11 actors. 6 males, 5 females.   ****A Latino-themed play****

A Latino student is chosen at the last minute to join a humanitarian group from his school that is headed to Guatemala. But since his Spanish is weak, he faces ridicule and criticism from certain peers. Jealousy and anger trickle throughout the campus as the trip approaches, and the social buzz of the high school becomes even more hectic when the student's trip money is stolen on campus, jeopardizing his trip.

Stravinsky's Kitchen

Comedy. **High School/College.** 12-15 minutes. 3 actors: 3 males (or females).

Two friends secretly enter the home of an employer to obtain a forgotten object but the homeowner abruptly arrives home while they are there. As they hide in the kitchen's pantry and plot their getaway, the two talk and eventually argue, exposing the true colors of one of them. Upon their hasty exit a mistake is made, and one of them capitalizes on this mistake, resulting in his/her fortune.

Forty Whacks

Drama. Spooky. **High School/College.** 25-35 minutes. 3 actors: 2 females, 1 male.

A pair of siblings have inherited the Lizzie Borden Bed and Breakfast in New England. Although the business was run for decades in a quiet, respectable fashion, one of the siblings is over-ambitious, wanting to unearth an alleged piece of buried evidence within the house. This brings about a chilly tension between brother and sister, and perhaps within the house itself.

John Calhoun and a Thief

Drama. **College.** 35-40 minutes. 3 actors: 2 females, 1 male.

Kicked out of a university PhD program, a bitter and dejected female lifts from the library archives original copies of John Calhoun's personal documents. Counseled and consoled by her roommates, her conscience slowly gets to her; but as she seeks entry to other universities her luck turns to worse, and the subsequent decisions she makes regarding the historic papers cause this one-act play to become darker, if not funnier.

Honoring the Hijacker

Drama. **College.** 12-15 minutes. 4 actors: 2 females, 2 males.

It's 1981, the ten-year anniversary of the famed hijacker D.B. Cooper. The play's four characters are attending a "D.B. Festival" and have stayed up very late, outlasting everybody else. The late night chit-chat goes from pranks and jokes to outright volatility, and suddenly this get-together becomes something that three of the four characters didn't bargain for.

It's a Super Day at Sammy's!

Comedy. **Middle or High School.** 35-40 minutes. 9 actors: 5 females, 4 males (4 possible adults).

Jodi has found a summer job at a travel agency. But her three younger siblings can't seem to live without her! They call her at the office incessantly, which interferes with the work. The standard telephone greeting "It's a super day at Sammy's!" becomes a repeated theme of this comedy, as Jodi struggles to reach a balance between her job and her nagging siblings

Three Tenners

Comedy/Drama. **Elementary through High School.** Three Ten-Minute Plays.

Three Creepy Plays

Drama. **Middle School through College.** Three short 'creepy' plays.

Hockey Masks in Hueytown

Drama. Spooky. **High School/College.** 20-25
minutes. 4 actors: 2 males, 2 females.

Driving home for Thanksgiving break, four college
students stop off in a small rural town to retrieve one
of the student's old family pictures. They reluctantly
enter the empty home of his deceased uncle, a former
producer for the Friday the 13th movies. Strange
objects are found during their search . . but when a
hockey mask surfaces, everything really goes
sideways.

The Witch Makes Five

Drama. Spooky. **High School.** 10 minutes. 4 actors: 2
males, 2 females.

After a bizarre group camping trip, a student is
checked into a youth mental facility . When she is
visited by the other members of the trip, memories of
the weekend trickle out . . . and horrific things begin to
happen.

Mrs. Calapooza and the Culebra

Dramedy. **Grades 5-8.** 10 minutes. 5 actors: 3 females, 2 males.

Fed up with their grouchy teacher's classroom ways, four students complain and bicker back and forth during a Spanish quiz. The situation grows worse when the friends discover that one of them has pulled the ultimate prank on the teacher.

Raiders of the Lost Rakasa

Dramedy. **Grades 5-8.** 10 minutes. 7 actors: 4 females, 3 males.

Seven young explorers arrive at a cave in a far-off land in search of the great "Rakasa." They find what they want . . . along with a few of the cave's unexpected surprises.